# Of
# Mineral

# Tiff
# Dressen

Nightboat Books
New York

# Of
# Mineral

# Tiff
# Dressen

ISBN: 978-1-64362-141-8

Design and typesetting by Rissa Hochberger
Typeset in Century Schoolbook and Chronicle Display

Cataloging-in-publication data is available from the
Library of Congress

Nightboat Books
New York
www.nightboat.org

# Table of Contents

*in memory of Colleen Lookingbill*

Once in a city block and filled, I saw
the light lie in the deep chasm of a street,
palpable and blue, as though it had drifted in
from say, the sea, a purity of space.


—William Bronk

## Theirs

Anything but crinoline

dressed estrogen
fetish.   God how I

just kissed
lust mistook

nascent opulence
pissed queer
resistance stood

tacit under violet

windchimes.

X.

Yoked for zero
gravity.

# A Letter in May: from Portola, San Francisco

This city is a labyrinth
I walk     in my head
another poet repeats:

> "there is no space left in America,
> there is only distance"

~~~~

last night in corpse pose

> I thought of the corpse
> flower death camas
> lily-of-the-valley

this morning I dreamt
> a single many-petaled
> bloom emerged
> from my thigh
> you wanted
> to name my new
> flower.

~~~~

This city is a labyrinth

      I walk in my they/body

                            Anders als die Andern

      past the international church
              of the foursquare gospel

      up the water

      tower the bee
            *Whose flowers are flames*

      *lit to the Lady*

      from the rabbi
           to herbalist

               past the vanished

                 consulate of Malta

      the Avenue Theater marquee
      says "The little neighborhood
          that could"

How do I

create the distance

you need

to reach across?

~~~~

Looking out the bedroom window

I repeat after you *pinus pinea*

umbrella pine Italian stone pine

parasol pine

I ask: *how* is it possible

that we can see    the Salesforce tower

from here?

This morning I carried

Briquette downstairs

to her sun spot

her malleable feline

creatureness

comfort-in-mass the
weight of those
I love   upon me




~~~~



This city is a labyrinth


I walk
in my invasive/species body

*wherefrom the shadows*
*that are forms fall*



where people forget you
in time

Itasca
Odessa

pushed up against
Fleetwood
Travel Queen


7

        this edge
           of reservoir


Underneath the *arbutus unedo* Irish


Strawberry tree
      "to the tragedy of vehicular homelessness"

           the cain apple




You are part of the city

      the city will forget




          ~~~~



I've learned where to walk
      along the structural
      scars of
      a city

*Wherefrom fall all architectures I am*

                    awakened in subduction
                    zoned
                    lost
                    under the 101




            squatting in this skeletal
            green-


                    house with phantom
                    flower crops

                    "It's still warmer here"

## Poem for April 2014
*after Frank O'Hara*

after noon
light drops
this blood
orange flesh
window it is
late april and
snowing still
in the part
of the world
I come from
vascular
roots of desire
what is the
purpose of
desire? small
animals live and
die in the
brushes nearby
I walk through
the rosemary to
smell the rosemary
I can't see
your face anymore
where you should
have been I
see peonies

I am watching
a film in
my head I call:
*I don't know how to get*
*from country "discipline" to*
*territory "surrender"*
bleeding to death isn't
so bad is it?
what if it all
came out blue
like persian indigo?
would that frighten you?

## Poem for Epiphany #1
*after John Wieners*

I rest my head on
the sundial
I know there are
things for the sole
purpose of forgetting
I forget them
then patiently
finally I was back
on the vertical
I was blue smoke up
the chimney apparition
rose paper sand
piper please ignite
a new structure
for love why don't
you while you're at it
red and bright and
holy like the honey-
tuned clockworks in
your eyes the day
steals from me.

## Poem for Epiphany #2
*in memory of Justin Kane*

I walk the first
scars on snow
all the night
bright over
brittle I am sky-
illiterate that story
in which she
sold her hair
magicians star-
diviners
bird nests
naked deciduous
I spent the night
sugar pines
drop saying
goodbye
the largest cones
I can recall
he was gifted
with animals
may have even
spoken animal
with his hands
I thought if only
I could see
Saturn's rings.

In a red
transient nightgown
or astral caul
you are still divided from me
at the instance of our arrival


—Kimberly Lyons

<u>Dark Sky Preserves</u>

Because I wanted to learn how
to look at the sky
         again

        I chose from among
        your voices
                constellations

                nuclear
      magic
                    numbers

I began believing

        in a we who are faintest
           at the zenith

           When I found you
                listening in a whispering
              gallery

           marine and
              terrestrial

        your whole body
           a tongue

I believed in
                your life
                                bearing songs


in stalactite time scale
                in helium articulate reverence
                        and reservoirs over




~~~~




Because you said the sky
                is a kind of ocean



                we learned the alchemy
                        of air
                        we became many

Do we *have* dreams or
                    do we *see* them?



Do you know the feeling
          in music
                    where possession
                    before it leaves you
                              from pressure or
                              percussion?



Because there will always be
          light trespass


                              we made dark sky
                              preserves



because we could treat
                    the darkness as
                    property

Because I wanted to feel the air
                    visible breath
                                eternal ice


            in a cyclone        you said


                    I sing over you
                    while you sleep


            I will curate
                    your dreaming
                        your sun-lions and
            your chariot
                        drawn by the sun

## Aria begins
(or poem for "thou unnecessary letter")
*for Barbara Guest*


Aria begins


    count    decahedron's


              echo

                    finite guest


     headlamp illuminations


  kaleidoscopic
         lung-wreck


     marigold     nebulae


        O Monde!


        Omega



(parallel          questions        rendezvous)

serpentine

timescales


waif-form

xeroxed


yesterday's

zed.

## Fugue: a poem for multiple voices
### for Alan Turing (1912-1954)

It's only sounds in a mathematical series yet
human beings are so moved by it. What gives it
this magic: the composer or the instrument? Is
the magic in me? Or in those who feel emotion
when they hear what I play? I can understand
this emotion but I am unable to share it. I am
intrigued by the music, but it means nothing
more to me.

—Rantes on playing Bach in Eliseo Subiela's
film *Man Facing Southeast* (Argentina 1986)

Being holy  ographic

      our human suffering

being what we
claim to be

      What is hagiography?

            an image projected onto
                  earth in the image of?

"Only sounds in a

            mathematical series"

            imagine we are
                all canonical

        those of us who
                make projections

Upon arrival I was
space      the lens itself

in which you are always
an object waiting to be

viewed   upon   mass   speck
contained in asylum contained in astral
courtyard alien quarry


Upon arrival I was
the instrument playing
the mind that people hear

*Now there's a space to fill*
*with you in it*
*a space in which to be found*
*and you will be found*

When he said computer

    he meant the human
        mind at work on an

    empirical human

    problem

Someone said empathy   the measure

    of emotion  available

        in an open
        system
        to do work

           for others

When did words cease
      and code become

      greater than
          or equal
          to flesh?


I have heard that
      the "set of all sets" could be
      self-contradictory



If we gather together
      the right lobe in the left
      hand walking
          backwards into
          the sea

We are all
        speaking parts


We are all responders
as if we could have been
        anything but illogical
structures resembling bodies
fired in medicinal
        ovens


We are all transponders
as if we could have been
        anything but corporeal
        collaborators

Even though the flesh kept
                        dying we made

overtures to every organ
                in our bodies


If only we had
        bodies we could be
        found   if there were


        short wave sounds
    we could wrap ourselves
        around

Bach
transmitting
a
fugue


Who becomes a
*thinking* creature
coiled into
a snail's
shell


I am at least five
times the image
removed

Seraphic doctor translator
of relics
transistors


Encrypt this body
in solid state
enigma


We are born
of ash from human(ed)
flesh


We are the hue of

amended ash


A pint of blue I gave to you
A pint of blue blood

A gift to thee

A firecracker in each
        hand a human shell he
          lit hell he


Let light pass through
        slits in an opaque
          screen


        All strings of the same
          length tuned to the same


Inside a skull   wind-
        plucked and
            placed
      on a sill

Do we reach the sea with clocks
In our pockets, with the noise of the sea
In the sea, or are we carriers
Of a purer and more silent water?


—Paul Éluard

# Night Ark: Poem in October
## *after Karin Lessing*

Sea starved
we begin with
motion liquid oar
we took on water
night phospho
reticence
under pole
star plunge
some fish spoke
through my
lungs some large
mammal bellow
who is native
and who is not
those who could
swim survived
we studied those
tiny forces.

## deep July, what Heraclitus said

minnow-speak
I hide among the
fin bodies beneath
and wait

      what are you in your
surface    dreams    chemistry
metamorphic swimmer
        ephemeraoptera?

          the sun scales we
abandon lures we
      decompose in a
different language

## Earth's Body

Could I not at random enter all, enter you openly
        into her self or his self, or the mother and
        father of selves, enter bedrock,

the silvered edge
        sibilance,

diluvial medium of me—this speech secreted

I close your eyes, I hear the colors

of earth at large through
  exhaust pipes, through the precise
  ore picked from bone
  or the wild-root ascendant
  nearest me,


we are of the same lineage

of the still-warm oven-bird picked
        from the sewer grate
        to carry in your
        cupped hands

your offering
        your metabolizing
        dream-body that eats night
        air because it is a
        tangible thing

of the words we found, they were light


                enough for tilling

dissolving medium of me,
      close your eyes
      you are bleeding out
      into a bright helium night, in which
      I tuned you


harpsichord by the sea

be a thousand sleeping

fish, "be ink thrown under the hull,"

be the fruit that ascends
          from the last tree
          you looked so intent at,

we were denied the original
          forest that grew here we
          claim space, light, water
          and fail

be the scarlet pollen
in amber,

"the first thread coming
out of the fleece trapped

in vegetation"

be the thread

bare resemblance

diluvial medium of me, a "rain of forms"
       comes over me,

there are bones in the river
       bed you touch me

where two

       rivulets meet.

# Starflower

1.

I turn my
back

yard face

my cat
crawls

under
borage

lit to blooms

to fuel

star
fever

that blood
orange sun

I forget what
to hearth

2.

From Taos, New Mexico a friend writes

*It's yellow season here*
                              beyond assembly lines


*between the sunflowers*
                    and fulfillment centers


                              *and the rabbitbrush*


In my mind I'm
turning over

                    the crypto economy


                              to rot
                              to flower
                                    fuel

3.

I bend to touch
    the scabiosa
        and go sub
        rosa


        desire is
feeling with
    roots and dissolving
        in rain


        grounded as
          calcium
  split as water
    silica and magnesium


  is release to
  the lithosphere

4.

I want to see the fields through
    optically thin clouds

                striations on their crystal
                          faces

  the lighter isotope
      pushed up
      against the continental
           shelf

                I want
                to be matter
                buried at
                sea

5.

I forget
what to
hearth
I remember
this orange
sun   that

bloodfever star
these blooms
lit to borage

my cat face

I crawl under

this yard I turn

my back on

6.

we could eat

these small blue

petals

## Poem for March 2020

Air   aerie

480 million alveoli


at the end
of bronchial


tubes
ghosted

nucleic
acids

We are only
shadow
patients


looking out
windows

corvids mourn their
own too

I try to pick out
song
sparrows

from the backyard
chorus   abundant

*Melospiza melodia*
adapting

cytokine
storms will
wash
over
inside us

the first of ten
as water to blood

Your morning bird report:

                the towhees prefer
                            mealworms

It's Saturday, the 28th

                        a hawk floats

                                over us

## Holy Week: April 2020

The city is a kind of sea, with hilltop islands
of wild space.

—Philosopher's Way,
McLaren Park, San Francisco

Above Visitacion Valley
                    a coyote sniffs
                                the air

All anyone ever

        has left is

            until that's gone

                    We watch each other

I lie down
        where the hummingbird
                sage spikes the open
                        slope

"A very large crowd had
                spread their cloaks
                        on the road,

others cut branches

from the trees"

sometimes I pick out the

places where I'd like to

They brought myrtle

willow and palm to their

makeshift shelters

Today's count 83,374

tidy tips lupine

and gold fields    try to remember

a time when you felt

calm

The Juno spacecraft

reports

"countless swirling,

hallucinatory

clouds of storms"

Atomic cycles of
            it's hard to say    life    continue


                    You open a bag
                            of bird seed


        and pour into
                the swaying dish

## Abecedary: in four parts
*after Inger Christensen*


1.


    alms blood

               adam of

                    iron melted

                          once

               inside us


           cobalt

               bombs    salted

               earth


                     I watched

              dendritic elder

        flowers   psalm

            a path I call

        Fibonacci's grace


    because "your teeth and

bones once

    were coral"

        hydrocarbons and

the ice age

2.

June nights kingdom come
    thy will be
    in the Carboniferous
    forests

            as in livestock
            melancholy as in

      "We might half-hope to find the animals
      In the sheds of a nation
      Kneeling at midnight,"

3.

Novas    optic
                nerve

                        somewhere in between

        we are plucked
        orange
        spots    minerals
                        in transit
                        nasturtium bright

4.

Can we predict
                quantum
                        restitution
        call it karma


                        call it my stolen
                                tender-loined


                under-the-wire


                        violet wound I was
    saving for another in


        carnation anew xeno


            yearning zenith

## Acknowledgements

My gratitude to my partner in life and adventure, Kate Sims, who's been a first audience for many of these poems. My deepest thanks to the QYD posse, Alex Mattraw, Tod Edgerton, and Megan Breiseth, whose critical guidance and feedback made this book possible, and to Joe Noble, Todd Melicker and Steve Hemenway for their ongoing encouragement and friendship. My thanks to Valerie Coulton and Ed Smallfield for all they do to create poetry community around the world. My gratitude to Nightboat Books for being an awesome press to work with!

# Notes on the Text

"there is no space left in America, there is only distance" from *A Letter at Easter: to George Stanley* by Beverly Dahlen.

"Whose flowers are flames/lit to the lady" and "wherefrom the shadows that are forms fall./ Wherefrom fall all architectures I am" from "Often I am Permitted to Return to a Meadow" by Robert Duncan.

"Thou unnecessary letter" (the zed) spoken from Kent to Oswald in Shakespeare's *King Lear*.

"A very large crowd had spread their cloaks on the road, others cut branches from trees." from Matthew 21:8.

"Now there's a space to fill/with you in it/a space in which to be found/and you will be found" from Ramsay Bell Breslin.

"be ink thrown under the hull" and "a rain of forms" from *707 Scott Street: The Journal of John Wieners* by John Wieners.

"The first thread coming/out of the fleece trapped/in vegetation" from Cecilia Vicuña's *Unravelling Words & the Weaving of Water*.

"your teeth and bones once were coral" from the essay "Lake Superior Country" by Lorine Niedecker.

"We might half-hope to find the animals/In the sheds of a nation/Kneeling at midnight" from "Of Being Numerous" by George Oppen.

"Fugue: a poem for multiple voices" features voices both living and deceased. One prominent voice (or spirit passing through) belongs to Alan Turing, mathematician, father of modern computer science, and WWII cryptographer primarily responsible for cracking the Enigma, the powerful Nazi cipher machine. His life was short and painful. Forced to undergo estrogen therapy as a "cure" for his homosexuality, he died by (allegedly) committing suicide by eating an apple laced with cyanide (perhaps to evoke another great mathematical mind, Sir Isaac Newton?).

A second prominent voice is that of Rantes, the protagonist of Eliseo Subiela's 1986 Argentinean film, "Man Facing Southeast." Rantes appears mysteriously one morning in a psychiatric hospital in Buenos Aires and claims he's an alien, something like a walking and breathing image, something like a living hologram projected from another planet. In character, he is very much saint/Christ like and, like Turing, is forced to undergo a chemical crucifixion. Also of interest in this film is the notion of code (in lieu of, or perhaps in addition to, the word or λογος) becoming flesh. What if logos has extended or evolved to include the possibility of binary code? What happens when a master of code, like Alan Turing, meets a literal and figurative code, embodied by someone like Rantes?

"Night Ark: Poem in October," "Poem for March 2020," and "Holy Week: April 2020" recently appeared in the journal *Parentheses, issue 4* Fall 2020. An earlier version of "Earth's Body" was published in *YewJournal*, Summer 2016.

"Dark Sky Preserves" and "Aria begins" appeared in http://mondaynightlit.com/ Spring 2020.

"Poem for April," "Poem for the Feast of the Epiphany," and "Poem in May: from Portola, San Francisco" were published in *ELDERLY 29: SO DIVINE,* issue 29 May 2019.

An earlier version of "Fugue: a poem for multiple voices" appeared in the chapbook *for Aeolus, variations on the element* co-published by the g.e. collective and Poetry Flash, San Francisco 2010.

Tiff Dressen's first book of poems *Songs from the Astral Bestiary* was published in 2014. In 2019, they played the role of Earl of Kent in a production of King Lear. They enjoy urban flâneuring, their felines, and setting type and printing at the San Francisco Center for the Book.

# NIGHTBOAT BOOKS

Nightboat Books, a nonprofit organization, seeks to develop audiences for writers whose work resists convention and transcends boundaries. We publish books rich with poignancy, intelligence, and risk. Please visit nightboat.org to learn about our titles and how you can support our future publications.

The following individuals have supported the publication of this book. We thank them for their generosity and commitment to the mission of Nightboat Books:

Anonymous (4)
Abraham Avnisan
Jean C. Ballantyne
The Robert C. Brooks Revocable Trust
Amanda Greenberger
Rachel Lithgow
Anne Marie Macari
Elizabeth Madans
Elizabeth Motika
Thomas Shardlow
Benjamin Taylor
Jerrie Whitfield & Richard Motika

This book is made possible, in part, by grants from the New York City Department of Cultural Affairs in partnership with the City Council, the New York State Council on the Arts Literature Program, and the Topanga Fund, which is dedicated to promoting the arts and literature of California.